Poems from 86th Street

Published by Orange Hat Publishing 2021
ISBN 9781645382614

Copyrighted © 2021 by Franklin Elementary School
All Rights Reserved
Poems from 86th Street
Second Edition
Written by Franklin Elementary School Students & Teachers
Illustrated by Franklin Elementary School Students & Teachers

All Rights Reserved. Written permission must be secured from the publisher to use or reproduce any part of this book, except for brief quotations in critical reviews or articles.

For information, please contact:
Orange Hat Publishing
www.orangehatpublishing.com
Waukesha, WI

For kids all over the world. Be proud of who you are. Believe in yourself. Celebrate you!

"Stay Positive"

"Believe in yourself!"

"be nice to freinds"

I Am... Poems

I am

by: g.s.

I am 8.
I am fansey Like a priinsess.
Bling Bling Bling.
I am kind Like a Dolfin.
I am prity Like a cat.
I am Hlpful.
I am ooreges.
Risk Risk Risk.
I am a shef.
2121212121.
I am me.
me m-e m-e.

School is the best school. School is fun.

School. School nuo.

I am...
By: A.B.N.

I am strong bam/and sometimes week.

I am active by doing taekwondo.

I am tired by doing school... yawn.

I am creativ by doing art.

I am nice thank you.

I am a friend... hello.

I am a boy.

I am me.

I am...
BY: ADAM

I am ADAM.
I am a 7 year old boy.
I am cool because I am strong.
I am nice to everyone.
I am a happy boy.
I am a ninja... POW!
I am kind to my family.
I am special.

I am Aden

I have brown skin as a penut. I do not like chees. I am hansom. I do not like to be calld cute.

I am
By Alex

I am stroing like metul
I am lovd like a tigr
I am kwtk like the wind
I am kind
I am speshl
I am nise

I am Poem

by Alivia

I am a sister
my skin is vinila icecream
my hair is chociate ice cream
my eyes are green grass
I am a good redder
I am english
I am a good Listener
I am me

I am...
By: Anonymous

I am a gamer.
I am a son.
I am a kind boy.
I am a good frend.
I am a artist swish!!
I am a big brother.
I am a reader of Dog Man books.
I am a little brother too.
I am happy with my pets.
I am me.

I am...
By: A.R.H.

I am tall.
I am a gutar playr. Beat, Beat.
I am a vilinist!
I am a daner and singer. oh la la!
I am a sister.
I am fast. Swish!
I am a pet lover. woof!
I am me.

I am...
  By: Avery A.K.A. Ave

I'm a cat lover meow.
I'm a football player stomp
I'm a fast runer.
I'm a swimmer splash.
I'm a good boy clean clean clean.
I'm a good frend play play play.
I'm a nise big brother.
I'm me!

I am Bently

I luv to wach youtub.
I am a boe.
I am six.
I Play Mindknrft.
I plax Fortnit.
I love to be mysle.

I am
By Brandon

I am healthy.
My eye cole is oshin blue.
I am olwelys Happey.
My Hair is Blond like lemons
My Falmey is the Best.
My Falmey is cool.
I am 7
I am Brandon

Mr Self
Bryce.

I am stron like my dog.
My skin is vnilu iscrem.
My eyes are drok cholit.
My age is 7.
My hair is drke nite
I am brave like a nite

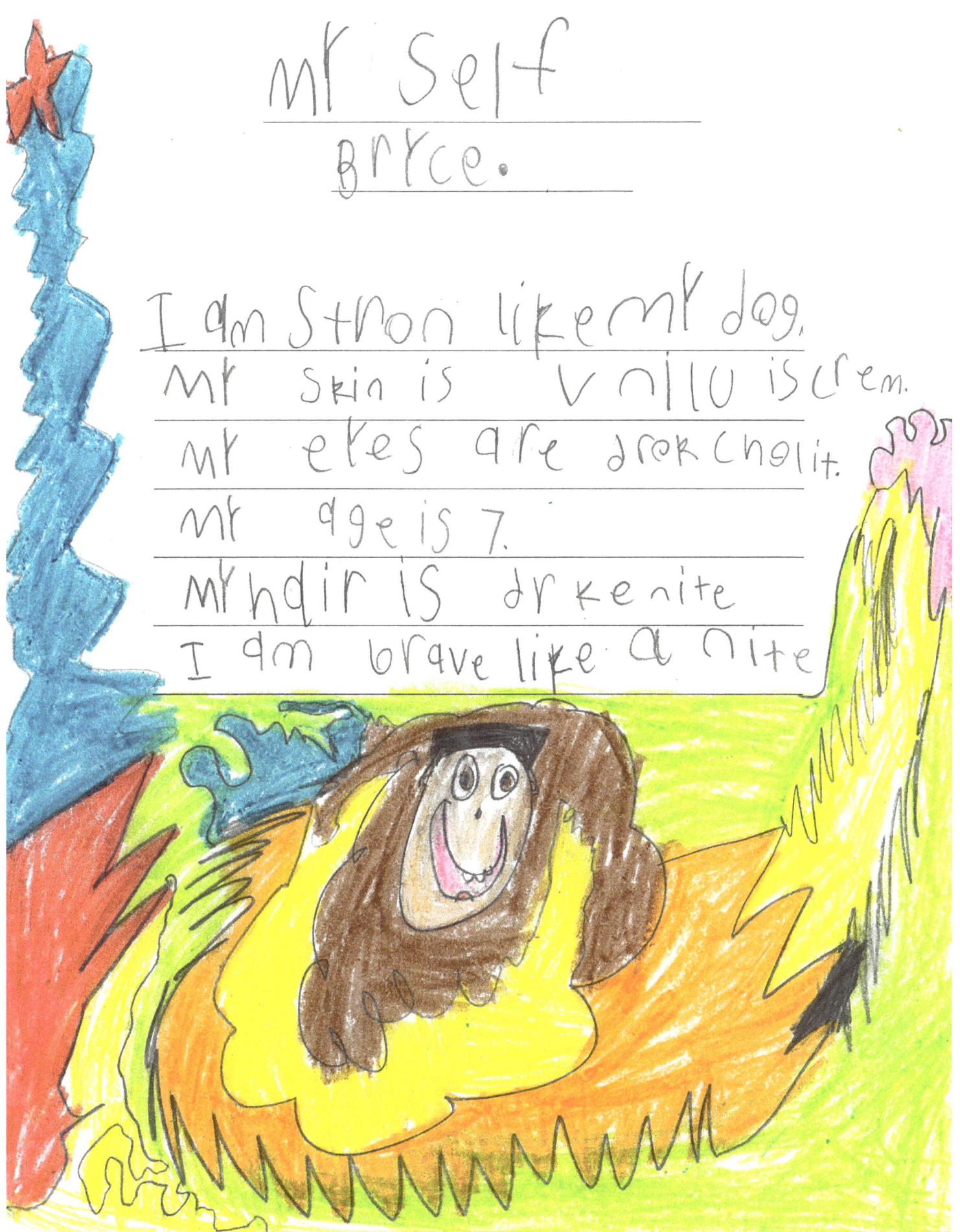

I AM
By Chase

I am strong.
Girl!
I am helpful.
Tall
I am caring.
I am sharing.
My eyes are as blue as the sea.

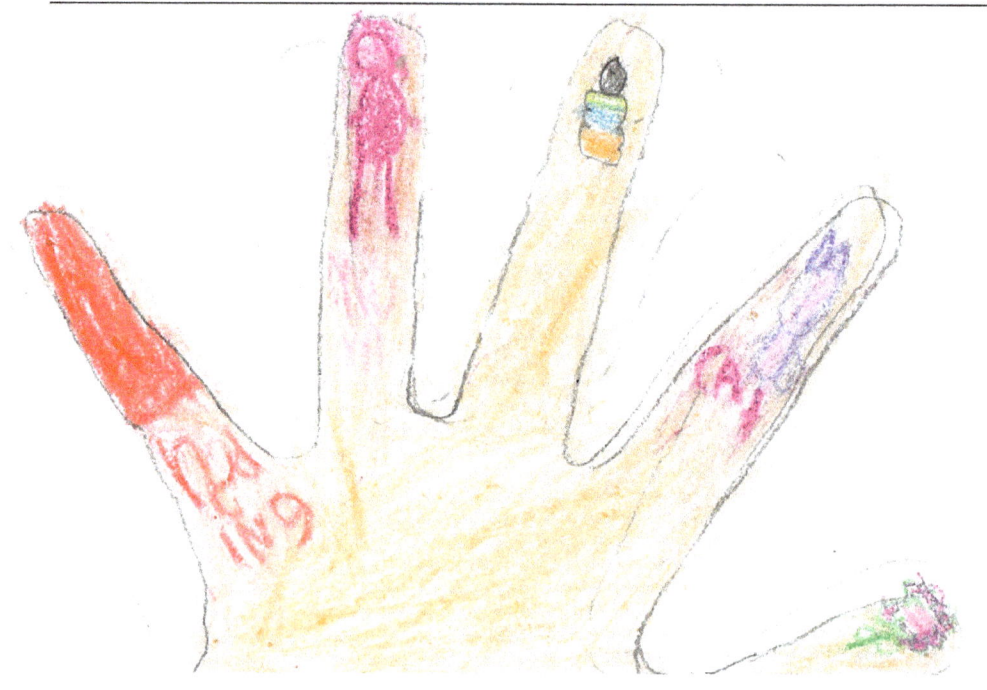

any one can be anything
by crewz Hoge

My skin is moon light as the sun flows.
My Hair is dark choclet it was so sweet.
Mom is hony do melon she is so com.
Dad is pie he is sweet and com to.
No one should get Jaged by there way.
I am spesnile to the whole world evrybodyis.
I am a gamer because I got insplerd to do it.
I am a beat boxer I got insperd so I did it.
my eyes are blue moon the moon lights them.
I am a gymnast, when my cousin did it I trid.
I am a flipper I did it because Ezra did.
I am a podcaster in first grade we did it.

I am...

By: Declyn

I am a relly good racer streeet.
I am 6 and a half years old almost 7)
I am a pritty good Parkour."
I am a boy with eyes like my dad
I am crazy.
I am a big and littel brother.
I am middel child.
I am a youTuber.

I am...
by: Deilali

I am a girl who loves Fluffy Puppy
I am a wild girl
I am a girl
I am a big and little sis
I am eight 7 years old and born in November
I am a gamer girl who plays Roblox
I am a girl with dark brown hair
I am me

I am
Dominique

I am black kind of brownish.
My hair is black.
I am six.
My family is grate.
I'am me.

My Poem
By Drake

I am nice, kind, Loving
I am funny fast like Flash
I'm cool a good friend
I like candy as much as Jace
I play video games like Super Mario
My eyes are blue like the ocean
I have a cat named Zio
I'm good at video games

I am Ema

I am a boe.
I like to piae.
I have tanish brownish skin.
I live wife me mom.

I Am...
By: Ernesto

I Am cool I Am loving
I Am smart I Am helpful
I Am kind I Am a seen
I Am son I Am brotter
I Am student I Am
I Am a I Am of I Am the
I Am me

I am...
By: E. W.

I am a devl4 swimmer!
I am a studnt.
I am a Girl yay!
I am a summer girl.
I am a math master.
I am me.

I am.
BY: Ezra

I am frenclly.
I am helpful.
I am famly.
I am a a boy with blue eyes.
I am a ccsin.
I am a frenci.
I am a alownsters nagnboy.
I am a baseball plaenwho.
I am a little brother
I am a minecraft gamer

I am Mrs. Garvey

I am kind and thoughtful.
I am funny.
I have hazel eyes and blonde hair.
I love my babies.
I wonder how my students are doing.
I try my best.
I want the sun to shine.
I make people happy.
I am Mrs. Garvey.

My Identity
By, Grayson. K

My famaliy is sun shine.
My hair is choclite.
My eyes are oceen watr.
My skin is wite choclite.
My haert is open.
I am me.

All about me!
By Hannah Geneclaywell

My skin is bright summery birch. My eyes are like the atlantick! My hair is creamy carimel bronse. And my wish is toFly! because them fix to school

I am...
By: Isaiah

I am a boy.
I am a good boy who is kind.
I am a cool boy.
I am a brave boy by not being scared.
I am a fine boy.
I am a little boy on the go.
I am a nice boy.
I am a boy with peachy gold skin.
I am a boy with sandy brown hair.
I am me.

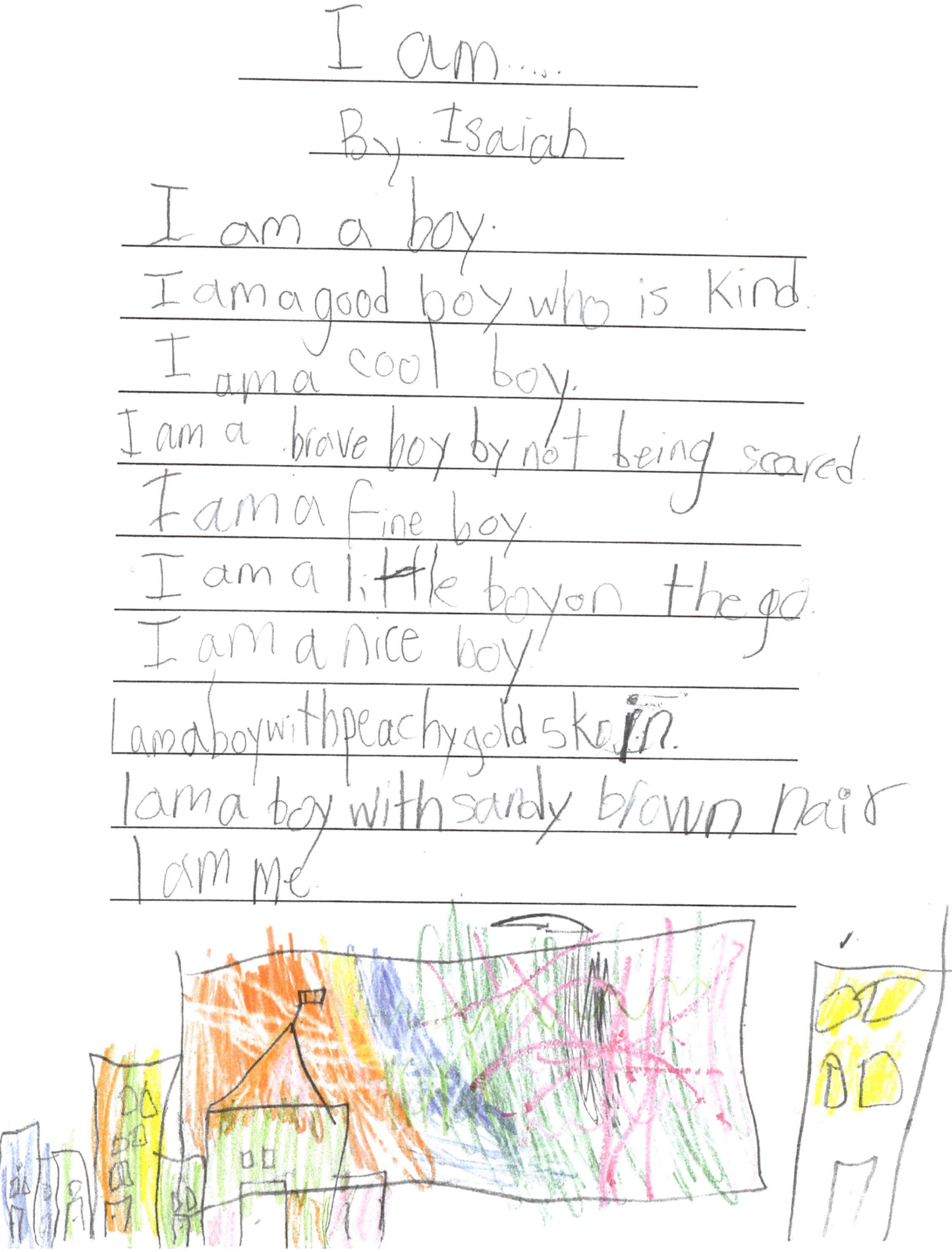

Jonathan
BY: J.O

I am kind.
I am eight years old.
My hair is like bark on a oak tree.
My skin is white birch tree.
My eyes are brown choclet.
I speak Englesh.
I am a gamer.
I am ME.

I AM
Jace

I am a kid.
I am shy.
I am loud.
I have blue EYES
I LIKE TO PLAY
PLAHTS vs. ZONBEZ

I am
Jackson

I am a boy.
I love my family.
I have brownish hair.
my eyes are blue like
the water.
I am seven.

I am Jasmine

I love love ice crem.
I am strong and powrful.
I am cring for people
I am sneke hehe
I love rainbows.
I love to play rodbox.
I love to go to the park.
I love skool

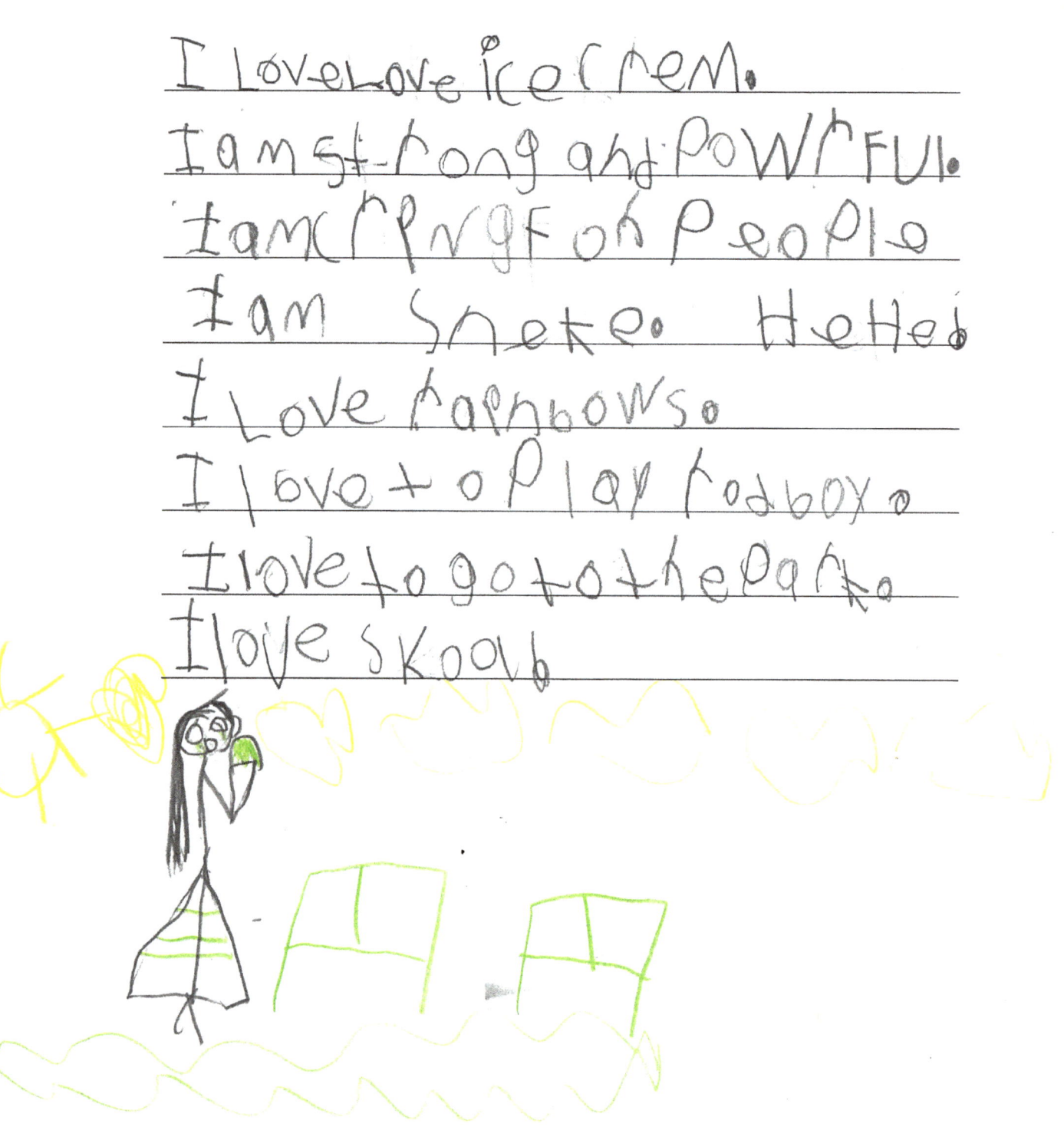

I am Jeremy
My head is like a rock. My hair is like grass. I am fast like a cheetah. I sleep like a panda. My skin is tan. I am scarred of poisonous snakes. I'm playful like a monkey.

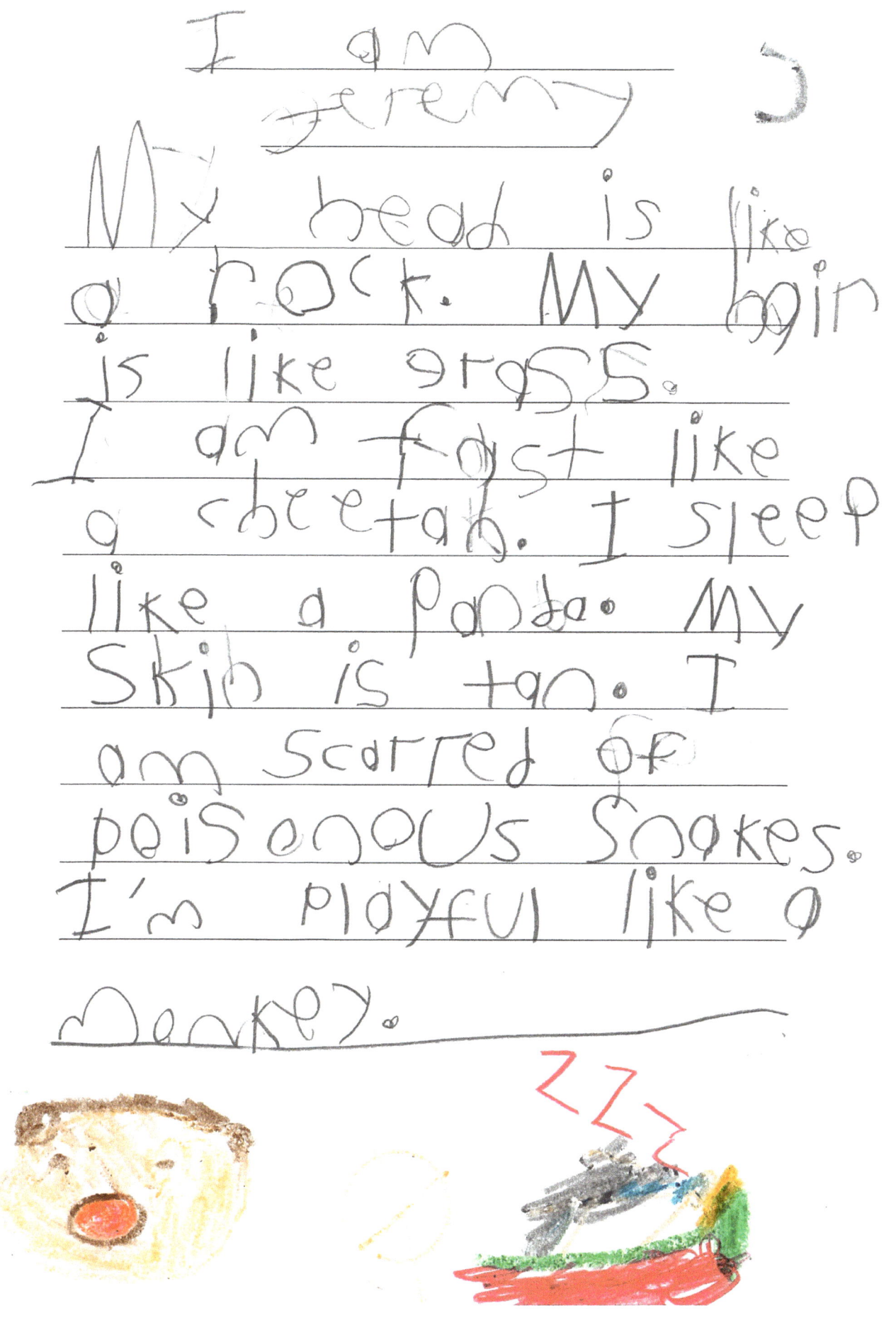

I Am
Jerome

I Am strong like a wave.
I Am kind like a heart.
I Am funny.
I Am happy.
My skin is light chocket.
My hair is like the night.
I Am Jerome

I Am
Ju

I am a little brownish, whitish tannish.
I am from Thailand!
I am a girl.
I speak English and Korin!

I am...
By: Kaiden

I am 7 years old
I am tall
I am nisce
I am grat at FotBall
I am Brown
I am Fast boy
I am a little brothr
I am Kaiden

I am...
By: Kaleb M.

I am a persoih how wahts to go to school evr day.
I am a persoih how wahts corona to go away.
I am a persoih how loues world.
I am a persoih how plays a gtat pluck.
I am a Ninteholo switch gamer boop pluck.
I am a tiger lover rooooor!
I am a Boy with apricot hair.
I am a littel brother.
I am White with eys like the osheah.
I am a ahimil rescur.
I am yuny like a fish.
I am me..

I Am Eli

- I am Eli
- I am Latvian and German and hope to go there someday
- I am Artistic and Creative and love to play with modeling clay
- I am scared of loud noises, especially alarms
- I am silly and love to laugh it's part of my charm.

- I am a Pisces and have the same Birthday as my sister
- I am bestfriends with Leddi and when she is gone I miss her
- I am ELI

I am power
I am Kenneth

I am kind
I am swet
I am resoefi
I am good
I am love
I am happy

I am...
By: K.I.N

I am Kristopher.
I am brev becos I am eveey theng.
I am A frend.
I am small becas I am me
I am farce becas that's how I am
I am a Boy
I am tiny brather
I am myself

I am...
B.K.M.K.

I am Kate.
I am grate at helping.
I am nise to people.
I am a big sister to Lucy.
I am strong.
I am brave.
I am a girl with blue eyes like mom
I am me

I am
By Leddi

I am Amaseng
I am crazy
I am a cook
I am Lejndare
I am creative
I am strong
I Love Animals
I am me
I am Leddi

I AM
By Henry

I am a happy boy
I am funny boy.
I am lego builder.
I am a good player.
I am a good brother.
I am a good reader.
short

I am me
By: Alana

I am 8
I am a gamer girl
I am girl color
I am beautiful
I am strong

I am
Lino

I am seven.
I am a boy.
My hair is black.
I like to have
fun with my family
I like to learn!

I am...

By: Logan

I am Logan.

I am 7, my birthday is July 31

I am someone who loves fruits

I am a apple lover crunch crunch.

I have brown hair and eyes like chocolate

I am someone who cites non broken stuff. shattered!!

I am a boy.

I am a person whos favorite game is Roblox

I am a blue color lover

I am a Ladingham

I am...
By: Luis

I am mportant.
I am loveing.
I am a little brother.
I am strong and happy party!
I am good at singing.
I am part of life.

I Am
Lyrik

I have litish
Brownish skin.
I have Black hare
like a walnut.
I have exes the color
of peanut Budr.

I am
malakai

I am six yers old.
I am going to be
sevpn. I have a big
bruther. I love my
mom and dad. I lkie to
play minacraft.

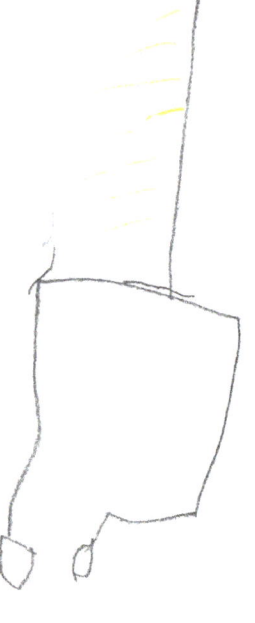

I am
Nathan Taylor

I like to sleep
I like to watch tovo at night
I like to be with my family at Wal-Mart
I like to stay home

I am Power

By nora joy

I am brave like a lion

I am fast like a cheeta

I am quiet like the wind

I am smart like a student

I am as nise as a dog

my hare is coliu'r brown

my sct rdup is wife rah

my vers is iine acs of rhr

I am nora joy

I am me!

I am
Mrs. O'Connor

I am a grown-up.
I am loud.
I am silly and kind.
I have pinkish whitish skin like a seashell
I have brown eyes and hair.
I am a teacher
I LOVE my family.
I am Mrs O'Connor

My Identity
Odin Walbert

I am as STRONG like a wreking ball
I am as loud as a lion
I am as Fast as my dad
My hare is as dreck as Chocolat
My eey aer like a oceen
I am Odin

I am...
By: Ms. Palkowski

I am a devoted mother to Alexander and Lauren.

I am excited when I see my students succeed.

I am generous with my heart.

I am happy when I am chosen to be someone's friend.

I am a true believer in serendipity.

I am comfortable being me.

I AM!
by: Mrs. Pritzl

I am strong!
I am brave!
I am also kind!
On different days, I use different ways to show just what I am. But every day in my heart, I am who I AM!

I Am
Ms. Romo

I am as sweet as pineapple.
I love to smile BIG.
I speak two languages.
I am hard working.
I love my family.
I am trustworthy.
I am calm like the wind.
I LOVE to go on adventures.
I am loving, honest, and optimistic. I am Ms. Romo!

Hello!

¡Hola!

I Am Me!
By: Mrs. Ruiz

I am funny.
I am kind.
I am shaping little minds.
I am helpful.
I am strong.
And my hair is very long!
I am patient.
I am smart.
I also have a very big heart!
I am Mrs. Ruiz.

I am
Ryan

I am a boy.
I have orangesh
wiytesh skin.
I have brown
eyes and brown
hair. I am me.

I am
By, S.G

 I am as quiet as the wind.
I am creative like a Paint brush
 I am porDercan ¡Hola!.
 I am 7.
I am smart like a student.
 I am a good singer Like Tayli Swift
I am tan like a wall.
 I am loud like rock and roll
I am focused.
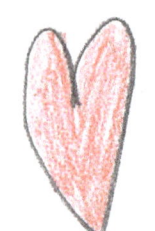 I am fast as a chita.
I am me!

I Am
By, Mrs. Schaefer

I am gentle rhythm and mellow song
Graceful and strong
I am mountain cliffs and ocean waves
Quiet and calm
I am sunny days and starry nights
Wishful and bright
I am many and I am one
I am me.

I am
Silas

I am a boy.
My skin is white.
My hair is blod.
I plant that is my job.
I am silly.
I am me.

Myself
By Stella

I am brave like an explorer.
My eye's are green like the jungle.
My hair is oak log.
I am loud like thunder.
My skin is sand and coconut.
My age gos like this. 1,2,3,4,5,6,7
I am me.
I am Stella.

I AM Skye
by S W C

My skin is like ocean sand
My hair is blond as the sun
My eyes are like a new leaf
My dada creme vinigr
Whipth a spreng cull of wipcreame
My mama is new fallen snow
Winth a spreng cull of wipcream
And a dash of viniu
I am smart + kind + rtest + outermen
I am 7 years old
I am Skye.
I am me.

I Am...
By: Sylvia

I am a kid.
I am a lucky girl!
I am a big sistr...xoxo
I am a cat lover
I am a dog lover
I am nice
I am Sylvia
I am me ♥

pup catunicorn ★ cat

I AM POEM
By Terrell

My skin is like a brown jacktree
My eyes is like Dark sand color
My Hair Black like chocolet Bar
I AM Me!!!
I AM Strong Like A Wave
I AM Terrell!!!

I am
by Tony. A

My eyes are like chocolate.
My skin is sand.
My hair is chocolate brown.
My skin is like the sun.
I am,
I am Tony.
I like dog.
I like cats.

I Am me.
Wyatt.

I am fun.
I Liked dog.
I spec eglish.
I luv mom and dad.
I like to play minecraft.
I Am 7.

I am...
Ms. Wilson

I am me.

I am brave like a honey badger.

I am determined like no other.

I am Polish and German in heritage.

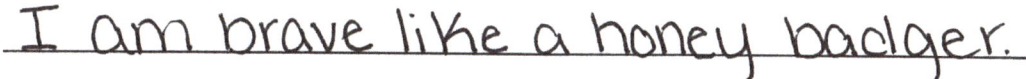

I am an educator who loves to learn.

I am a protective big sister to my brother.

I am an animal lover, awww!

I am a girl with eyes brown like dirt.

I am a girl with hair like carmels.

I am kind and loving to all I meet.

I am so much more than meets the eye...

I am me.

I am
Zaire

I am a boy.
I am six years old.
I am a first grader.
My hair is like a super rock star.
My skin is brown like an oak tree.
My eyes are brown like my mom's.
I am me!

Girl Powr

By: aaliya Lenora

Girls are girls.
Girls are generous.
Girls are nise.
Girls are asome.
Girls are cool.
Girls are Daring.
Girls are artistik.
Girls are amasing.

Heros
By: Boy Avengrs

Heros help in the community.
Heros help the perents.
Heros help the kids.
Heros help everyone.
Do you have one?
hind is your hero?

Team Work
by crewz and oden

Team work is helpful for evry one.
Team work is how YOU get friends.
Team work is helping some body.
Team work is kind to other's.
Team work is nice for other pepole.
team work is nice right?

help me!

Eyes
Collaborative Poem

Eyes are beautiful.
Eyes can be brown, blue, green or hazel.
We use our eyes to see.
Our eyes blink fast and slow.
Some people can keep their eyes open very long.
Eyes have eyelashes
Eyes can be tired like pandas.
Eyes are BEAUTIFUL!

Friends
By: DAA Boys

Friends are nice
Really respectful
care about friends
Evey friend is important
Not mean
Do fun things
Super great

Hobbies
By: Eble

Hobbies are something you do.
They're are something love.
Hobbies can be so many thing.
Games drawing reading...
You can do them in the morning.
You can do them at night.
You can do them wherever.
What's your hobby?

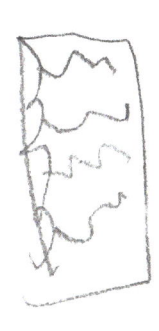

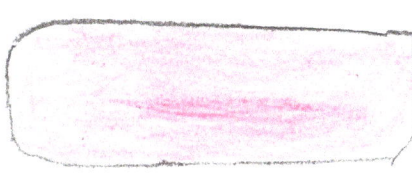

Hair
By: Girl Group

Some people have long hair.
Some people have curly hair.
Some people have different colored hair like a rainbow.
Some people have black hair as dark as when lights go off.
Some people have short hair.
Some people have really long hair as long as a snake.
Some people have no hair at all.

mom's
By Grayson.K. Kenneth. Odin

Are mom's are sweet like sheuan.
Mom's watch over us.
Are mom's take care of us.
Mom's are nice.
Mom's are as fun as can be.
Mom's are funny.
Mom's are Good.
Mom are awosome

All about hair
By Hannah, Alivia, Skye

Hair can be strait.
Hair can be curly.
Hair can be wavey.
Hair can be Afro!
Hair can be in all colors of the rainbow.
People can have no hair. Hair can show Expression!

Feeling Poem

By, Johnny, Brandon, Stella

I am happy when I play Roblox.
I am sad when I get hurt.
I am mad when people are mean.
I am suprised when I get toys.
I am tired when I have a long day.
I am shy when I join a new clas.
I am scared when I'm in the dark.
Feelings feelings feelings.

Black and White
by Johnny and Cruz

Some people are black,
Some people are white,
But there are no perks of being one or anote
You should not judge people by what they are
Because you will fell bad.
All people should be treated the sam

Kids Rock

By Johnny, Stella and Brandon

K is for kids.
I is for insperation.
D is for daring.
S is for studying.
R is for rock stars.
O is for open minded.
C is for cool kids.
K is for kind kids.

Family values
By: Marvel Fam

Different colors
Different ages
There always there for you
There are different styles
Step families and blended families
Help when you need it
Families are supportive
Families are important
Families have different feelings
Families make you smile

Home Sweet Home
By: Master Builders

Homes can look different
Homes are for families.
Holidays and birthdays
Help solve problems
Have dinner together
Holds memories

Age
by the night fairy dragon

People are old. People are young. People can be 7, 8, 10, or 50. Sometimes people live up to 100 years old. There's diffenent ages in families. You should love and respect your family, neighbors, and friends no matter the age.

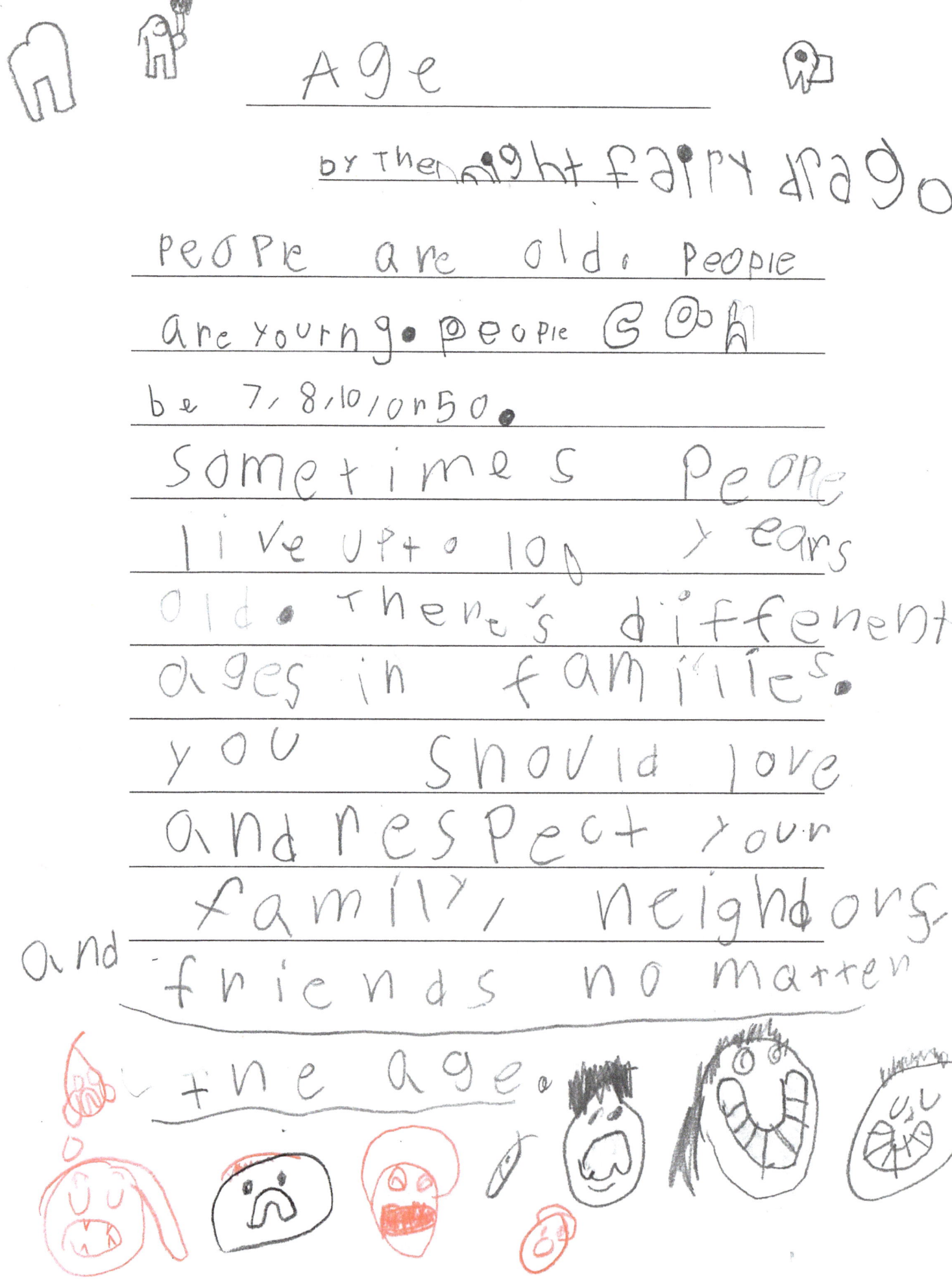

Differnt sizes
By: obby 15

Some people are small
Some people are tiny
Som people are big
Some people are very big
Some people are normal sized
All sizes are great
Some people are different s[izes]
And that's okay

Wearing a mask
by odin and crewz

Wearing a mask is good for the world.
Wearing a mask is good task.
Wearing a mask is good for people.
Wearing a mask is keeping you safe.
Wearing a mask is good for you.
Do you wear a mask?

Teachers Are

Ms. O'Connor, Ms Romo, Ms Ruiz class

Teachers are nice.
Teachers are different colors.
Teachers like to drink coffee in the morning, in the afternoon and at night!
Teachers are smart like scientists.
Teachers are helpful.
Teachers are funny.
Teachers work on their laptops.
Teachers are great!

We Are...
Roadrunners

We are creative

We are supportive

We are important

We are helpful

We all lose teeth as we grow!

We are all human beings!

We have different hairstyles

We have different eye colors

We have different communites

We have different families

We are all kind

We are all LOVED!

Skin Color

By the rockstars

Skin color can be black, white, tan, and brown. People can be different skin colors. Every skin color is good. Skin color is pretty on everyone. Skin color could look like something that you like. Brown like syrup. White like rice. Black like chocolate. Tan like a cracker.

All skin colors can be cool and beutiful.

Diffrent hair colrs

By Stella & Alivia

Dark Black hair as the night sky.
White Blond hair like carmul.
Dark Brown hair like chocolute ice crm
White hair like snow flakes.
Red hair like cherrys
Green hair like green grass.
Blue hair like the sky.
Pink hair like cotten cundy.
Teal hair like water.
Orange hair like a pumpkin.
Purple hair like grapes
Yellow hair like the sun.
Hair Hair everywhere

eyes and coler

By: soravan hannan skye.

Choclate brown, Green grape, Blueberry blue, Some Don't snow But there Bytifyl Like all of you, all eyes are the coler of the rainbow, All eye's are diffrent shapes and sises. Some eye's are rare. Some eye's are commen. Some just siung in the middel All eyes are dirrrent and

uniqe!

We are
By, Sorayan, Johnny, and Alivia

We are Albert Einstein smart.

We are good friends.

We are perfect the way we are.

We are loving.

We are happy.

We are cool like you.

We are different from each other.

We are kind.

We are kids.

We are strong.

Teachers

By, Mrs. Schaefer, Mrs. Ruiz, Mrs. O'Connor, Ms. Romo, Ms. Palkowski, Ms. Wilson

T is for talented teamwork.

E is for energetic, entertaining, enthusiastic.

A is for absolutely amazing.

C is for caring community.

H is for helping hands.

E is for encouraging elementary educators.

R is for reliable, rare, resilient.

S is for savvy spellers.

Our Identity
Kenzii Grayson

My skin is sand and my
friends skin is oak tree
My hair is milk cooklit and
my friends hair is dark cooklit
My eyes is ocuen blue
and my frinds eyes is dark brwn
We are strong like a wave
We are Kenzii and Grayson

Dads Are
Tony and Kenneth

Dads Are cool
Dads Are nice
Dads Are gamers
Dads rock
Dads Are neat
Dads Are right
Dads Are awesome
Dads Dads Dads

We love our dads!

To Mary Kenneth
We Are

We are cool.
We are gamers.
We are nice.
We are good.
We are people.
We are giving.

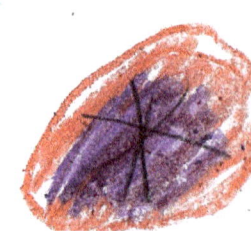

Names
By: working hand

What is your name?
Names tell people who you are.
People have different names.
they come from different places.
your name has moaning.
Everyone's name is special.
People need a name.
Names give you a name.
What is your name?
Everyone has a name...

www.ingramcontent.com/pod-product-compliance
Lightning Source LLC
LaVergne TN
LVHW070949070426
835507LV00030B/3466